The Best Medicine

ROSE RIGDEN'S
THE BEST MEDICINE

Published by Footloose Enterprises Limited
140C Woodcock Road, RD3,
Hamilton, 3283, New Zealand.
Email: sales@thenaturalselection.net
Website: www.thenaturalselection.net

ISBN 978-0-473-11863-1

THE ARTIST

Once again, Wildlife artist Rose Rigden shows her wry sense
of humour in the transposed relations between 'animals
and us'! Rose is an experienced Zimbabwean artist, exhibited
extensively throughout Southern Africa. She has gained
international recognition for work in design and formal art. Rose
lives with her husband in the 'Vumba' mountains on the Eastern
border of Zimbabwe.

In a fitting sequel to her best selling "WILDSIDE" Rose's "THE BEST MEDICINE" is the perfect pick-me-up to bring a smile to someone's face. Rose shows us that whatever form we take we all need a tonic from time to time. This refreshing perspective is a prescription proving that ...

No matter which way
   you take your treatment

Laughter is........THE BEST MEDICINE!

Some treatment may prove rough...

...and small doses may not be enough!

As humans, we share with all creatures great and small, common personality problems.

Sometimes we are serious... sometimes curious...

...and sometimes just plain cruel.

Sometimes sad...

We all, however, have a side to our natures, which in certain situations exposes our bad tempers.

WHAT THEN IS IT, THAT MAKES US LAUGH?

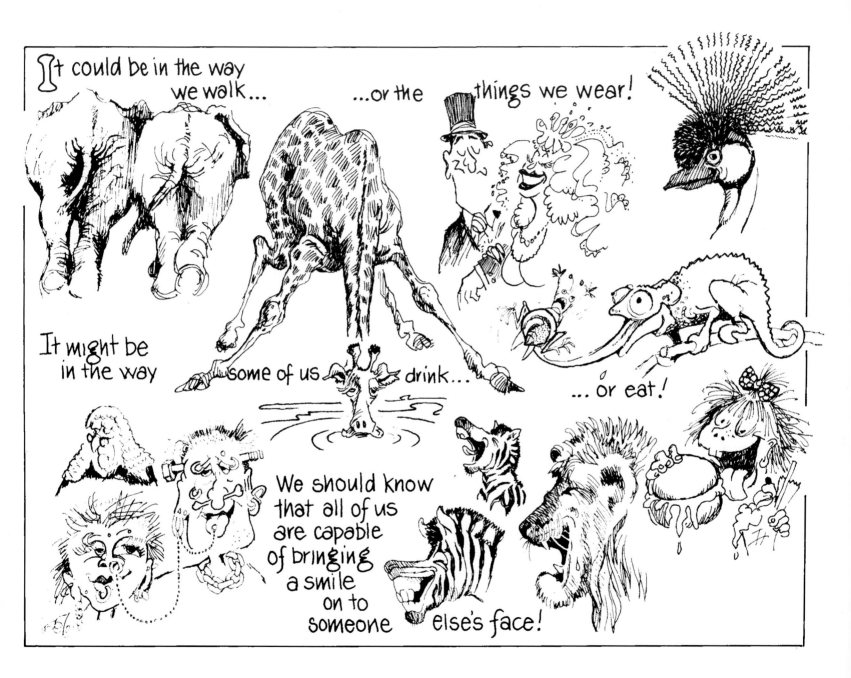

It could be in the way we walk... ...or the things we wear!

It might be in the way some of us drink... ...or eat!

We should know that all of us are capable of bringing a smile on to someone else's face!

Life can be annoying ...

... or full of surprises!

We either have too little ...

"I see Fred's still got his drinking problem!"

... or too much!

We are taught the 'art of good manners' ...

... but our offspring are often rebellious and unruly!

Sometimes we feel unwanted and unloved ...

... and this results in phobias and 'hang ups'!

We all increase in
numbers at an
alarming rate ...

... and there is a raw basic nature common to all species.

Our 'thick skins' harbour parasites for some ...

... and life's irritations for others.

Like us, animals are proud caring parents ...

... and we are all aware of of the 'survival of the fittest'.

FEEDING TIMES
8am – 8p.m.

We all have large appetites and to prove it ...

... we use modern technology to best advantage!

We must make our voices heard from time to time ...

... and be prepared for the worst!

We often re-locate ...

... if we can find the energy!

28   People generally stay in contact, in spite of family feuds ...

... and peaceful havens are often found in the middle of life's troubles!

Expect the unexpected ...

... and remember it's important to remain positive!

... we must always look our best!

We obey rules and regulations ...

... and exhibit tolerance to all.

Be kind to the older generations ...

... and have patience with the sick, lame and lazy!

... *even if it is only ‘NOISE’!*

We look for justice ...

We observe each other's behaviour ...

... which we imitate on the odd occasion!

On the surface, all may seem normal ...

... but sometimes it pays to take precautions!

46 Life sometimes appears ...

to be a big race!

We tend to relax when all is well.

Sometimes we are tempted on life's journey!

An innocent situation can have hidden agendas ...

51

We are reminded of our vulnerability ...

A level balance has to be kept ...

... not too far from the cutting edge.

Have enough space to enjoy life ...

... but keep your ears open for trouble!

Honesty is always ...

... the best policy!

Let's level the playing fields ...

... and keep up appearances.

Even when things go wrong ...

... we should take them in our stride.

Keeping up with the 'Jones' ...

... could change us forever!

We often see the 'animal in man' ...

"MOVE OVER A BIT HERB,
THOSE TREE TRUNKS
MAKE A NICE BACKGROUND"

67

68   **Man and beast have basic hostile tendencies ...**

... and our aggressive natures have to be controlled ...

We must trust each other ...

... and live in harmony!

We enjoy social benefits ...

74

... and swimming against the tide has its own perils.

We all make mistakes ...

We all look for love ...

... and sometimes get more than our share!

The trails of life are littered with failures ...

... but we press on regardless!

82   We try new ideas ...

... and try to 'shake off' old images!

Sometimes we vary our tastes ...

... and blame others

... and class distinction is never far away!

Striving toward our own goals ...

... we take the knocks!

... and keep out of trouble!

We must all be grateful ...

... even when things go wrong!

Just remember amidst all life's ills...and discomforts ...

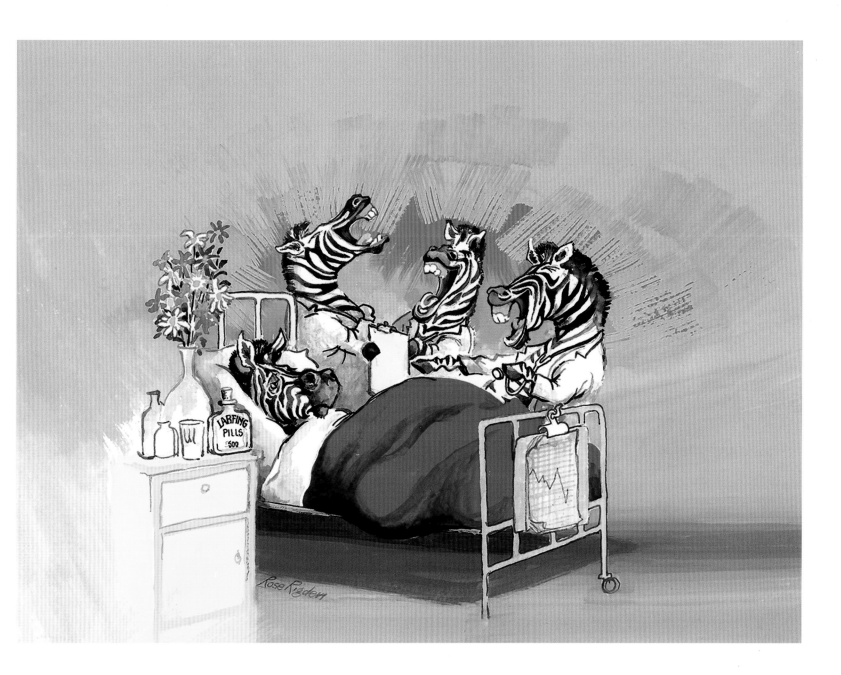

... 'LAUGHTER IS THE BEST MEDICINE'!

THE END